Americans Economy takes a new turn; The effect of the new inflation act on the Americans economy.

By

Kelvin B. Cowden

Copyright.

Table of contents

Prelouge : The beginning

The bill, known as the Inflation Reduction Act of 2022, gets the biggest ever speculation to handle environmental change, with generally $370 billion devoted to checking destructive discharges and advancing green innovation. The bill likewise moves to cover and lower seniors' medication costs while saving around 13 million low- and middle-income Americans from expansions in their insurance payments that in any case would happen one year from now.

The 220-to-207 vote denoted the perfection of about eighteen months of discussion that on occasion set the party's administrators in opposition to one another, particularly the Democrats' furious philosophical partitions. Eventually, however, the frequently irritable gathering grouped together to conquer consistent Republican resistance, taking on an action to further develop Americans' funds initially prefaced by Biden's 2020 mission promise to "work back better."

Democrats rely on updates to burden regulations to pay for the spending, which adds another base expense for billion-dollar partnerships that don't currently pay anything to the US government.This change, along with another new expense on stock buybacks and sharp subsidizing for the Internal Revenue Service to pursue charge cheats, is supposed to cover the bill's expenses.Liberals say it can likewise lessen the government's deficit by about $300 billion, but they still can't seem to outfit a last financial examination.

Chapter 1 ; The Inflation Act

The corporate least duty could have a negative impact on these extremely beneficial organizations.

The winding, turbulent way to entry started not long after Biden went into the White House. As the pandemic savaged the U.S. economy the previous spring, the president set forth a progression of strategy outlines that were meant to re-imagine the role of government in Americans' lives. Biden's arrangements left for all intents and purposes no part of the nation immaculate, trying to reexamine charge regulations, restore the country's maturing foundation, and spend huge aggregates on medical care, training, and the environment.

How a line of ongoing large-scale regulative successes moved Biden's administration In any case, is it past the time to influence the midterms? Leftists, in the long run, embraced a $1.9 trillion American Rescue Plan to answer the COVID last March, then tied down bipartisan help to put $1.2 trillion into the country's streets, spans, lines, ports, and web associations the previous fall. However, the president's party fought with itself in the months to follow over the last piece of Biden's plan, which designated government well-being net advantages and longer-term difficulties like an unnatural weather change.

It took a line of awkward public conflicts—apparently immovable battles between party dissidents and conservatives, including Sen. Joe Manchin III (W.Va.)—before Democratic pioneers arrived at a sensitive détente. The agreement reached last month primarily between Manchin and Senate Majority Leader Charles E. Schumer (N.Y.) forced party legislators to acknowledge what many saw as agonizing differences, as they had no choice but to abandon plans to expand Medicare, provide free general prekindergarten, and approve a slew of new guidelines for low-income families.

Yet, Democrats on Friday actually hailed the achievement, however impossible it once could have appeared, by focusing on how it follows through on a significant number of their past commitments.

"It's nothing that anyone would have said 90 days ago is plausible," House Speaker Nancy Pelosi (D-Calif.) said in a meeting, later emphasizing on the chamber floor that the bill "grows the commitment to wellbeing and financial security for a long time into the future."

The Liberals emitted an unruly adulation when they arrived at the expected voting section. Not long after that, Biden tweeted that he would sign it into regulation one week from now, saying: "Today, the American public won." Exceptional interests lost. "

The fourteen-day scramble that saved the Democrats' environment plan

House Republicans, in the mean time, mounted a firm, joined resistance. They went after the action as an expense increment on families, despite the fact that it doesn't raise people's rates. Furthermore, in their addresses, they demanded it would permit the public authorities to enlist a huge number of new IRS specialists to "nose about in your ledger, your Venmo, your private venture, and afterward the public authorities will shake you down for each and every penny," as House Minority Leader Kevin McCarthy (R-Calif.) said.

McCarthy's remarks — at one point portraying the "firearms" in the ownership of the assessment organization — misquoted the full reason for the proposed IRS reserves. In any case, he depicted the more full spending measure as the "most musically challenged bill" he had at any point seen.

"Today, individuals' homes ought to be attempting to answer our nation's call to address the rising cost of gas, food, and pretty much whatever else," McCarthy said.

For Democrats, the vote on Friday secured an achievement they had long regarded as critical to retaining their majority in November.Anything less than gambling irritated electors who were sold in 2020 on the commitment that Democrats would seek sensational monetary change. The triumph especially encouraged the party's dissidents, large numbers of whom guaranteed Friday to keep battling for the arrangements deserted for the sake of give and take.

"We demanded the Democratic larger part be conveyed," said Rep. Pramila Jayapal (D-Wash.), the head of the Congressional Progressive Caucus, a significant power in making the first $2 trillion proposition a year ago.

"We have won the contention for the president's full financial plan that we passed in the Build Back Better bill," she said at a news gathering. "Presently, we simply need a couple more Democratic congresspersons to make the remainder of that plan a reality."

Leftists are currently facing a challenge in selling the achievement at a time of mixed financial indicators and significant political vulnerability.Regardless of the labor market's continued solid growth, the threat of a downturn remains.Biden's fame is low in certain surveys, even after Democrats scored a wide exhibit of regulative triumphs lately, including regulations to limit firearm purchases, increase veterans' medical care and production of much-required central processors.

Adding to the test, another investigation delivered Friday by the Penn Wharton Budget Model offered a blended survey of the bill: The report found it would decrease the shortage by about $264 billion throughout the following ten years, not exactly a few Democrats' trust, with an impact on expansion that is "measurably undefined from nothing."

"Americans are languishing." Is it safe to say that we are here discussing how to reduce that misery? "No," said Rep. Jason T. Smith (Mo.), the top Republican on the House Budget Committee, adding the bill wouldn't "put out the fire of expansion."

The Senate supports the Inflation Reduction Act, securing long-postponed welfare and environmental bills.

Conservatives have recently proposed that a GOP majority in the next Congress try to roll back the regulation, as it did repeatedly with the Affordable

Care Act, which President Barack Obama signed into law in 2009.Rep. Steve Scalise (R-La.), the House minority whip, promised that for this present week his party would be "carrying out a plan that will turn around" the bill.

In any case, Democrats appear to invite such a danger. In a meeting with columnists on Thursday, a senior White House official said the result would assist the party with sharpening its new message to citizens: Democrats are helping customary Americans, while Republicans are radicals obligated to exceptional interests and the previous president, Donald Trump.

In the interim, Pelosi told The Washington Post that the impending races would offer Democrats a "major differentiation" from the GOP. She later added, "This is the way we're going on." The Republicans need to follow us off this way. "

The Inflation Reduction Act interestingly permits the U.S. government to arrange the cost of certain drugs for the benefit of seniors on Medicare—a clever framework set to produce results in 2026. The bill also covers these seniors' yearly personal remedy costs at $2,000 a year starting in 2025, and limits insulin co-pays to $35 beginning in 2023 for Medicare patients.

The proposition focuses on drug makers; it further forces punishments on those that raise the cost of Medicare recipients' prescriptions faster than the pace of expansion. While the "expansion refund" doesn't make a difference to solutions composed for Americans on confidential protection—a loss from the manner in which Democrats moved the bill in the Senate—legislators consider the action to be a significant triumph following quite a while of resolute drug industry resistance.

"However long I have been campaigning for office, individuals have been coming to me with worries about the cost of physician-endorsed drugs. The reality that I can say, 'We have heard you, we have moved forward,' is significant, "said Rep. Abigail Spanberger (D-Va.), a moderate running in a cutthroat race this November.

On environmental change, the bill appropriates $161 billion for new tax breaks to boost clean power and about $80 billion to urge shoppers to buy new or utilize electric vehicles and further develop the energy productivity of their homes. It likewise supports $1.5 billion to eliminate methane, a powerful ozone-depleting substance.

Various Republicans took to the floor Friday to attack Democrats' projects to respond to an Earth-wide temperature boost. Rep. Lauren Boebert (Colo.) at one point said legislators were "forfeiting American families in the special stepped area of environmental change."

Altogether, however, Democrats focused on their environment-related spending would decrease discharges by 40% under 2005 levels before the decade's over. What's more, they highlighted a heap of outrageous climate events as they presented the defense for forceful activity.

"The specialists are all saying we're exceptionally near the final turning point. On the off chance that we don't accomplish something soon, we probably won't have the option to save the planet, "said Rep. Robert C. "Bobby" Scott (D-Va.), administrator of the Education and Labor Committee.

To win Manchin's vote, be that as it may, Democrats a

Sen. Bernie Sanders (I-Vt.) — at long last, Democrats were able to secure a plan that allowed them to spend up to $3.5 trillion on their plan.

In the months to follow, each significant House council delivered reams of pages of administrative text toward the huge spending bill, which Democrats compared to the "Incomparable Society" changes sanctioned under Lyndon B. Johnson — a similarity Biden himself leaned toward. Their subsequent proposition planned to increase Medicare benefits, put billions of dollars into child care and free prekindergarten, approve new paid family and clinical leave, and increase government rates on rich Americans and partnerships.

However, their desires immediately crashed into the political reality. Nonconformists driven by Jayapal inclined toward sizable new government speculation while the party had intriguing control of Congress and the White House. Yet, they conflicted with moderates, including Manchin and Sinema, who took a more mindful financial view. Without each of the 50 Senate Democrats, the party had no real way to shepherd their bill through the chamber, leaving the discussion at a halt.

The pressures reached a critical stage in late September, as bombed talks slowed down the sum of Biden's regulative plan, including his foundation bill. That provoked an intriguing mediation from Biden, who made an individual enticement for his party on Capitol Hill to figure out some shared interest.

House Democrats ultimately chose a $2 trillion bundle, which they took on over GOP resistance in November. Yet, Manchin left it a month after the fact out of concern it could deteriorate expansion, chafing dissidents who felt the party had been kept prisoner by a sole exception. Indeed, even Biden, who once taught split the difference, communicated shock at the breakdown, igniting long periods of public killing between the White House and Manchin.

Talks continued this spring between the moderate West Virginian and Schumer, a bunch of seriously confidential conversations that frequently appeared to be nearly another failure. Indeed, even as Democrats slashed billions of dollars and slashed a portion of their most prized plans to help low-wage Americans, Manchin remained pained by the cost — and, at one point last month, abandoned the environment and duty strategies he had previously supported.

Be that as it may, Schumer and Manchin at last produced an arrangement before the month's over, opening the entryway for the Senate to embrace it this month. Pondering the trade-offs Democrats made just before the House vote, Pelosi said in a meeting that she had asked her individuals to "regard the bill for what it does" as opposed to "make decisions about it for what it doesn't."

"Yet, live to haggle further," she added.

Chapter 2;Effect of the act inflation act on our daily lives.

Wellbeing

The Fossil Fuel Byproducts Expansion Reduction Act aims to reduce the scarcity of fossil fuel byproducts.

On July 27, Sens. Chuck Schumer (D-N.Y.) and Joe Manchin (D-W.Va.) uncovered the Inflation Reduction Act (IRA), a spending plan compromise bill including a few key arrangements connected with the environment and energy, medical services, charge change, and shortfall decrease. The regulation is the result of months-long talks between Majority Leader Schumer and Senator Manchin following the passage of a section of the Build Back Better Act in the U.S. House before the end of last year.

As per a gauge from the fair Congressional Budget Office (CBO), the IRA would lessen government deficiencies by $102 billion somewhere in the range of 2022 and 2031—the life expectancy of the bill—through the execution of measures planned to diminish inflationary tensions.

As well as tending to the government's deficiency, the IRA expects to reduce fossil fuel byproducts by 40% under 2005 levels by 2030. It does as such by taking a huge interest in environmental and climate programs and giving duty motivators to support the turn of events and the organization of clean energy. A considerable lot of these projects incorporate direct financing, opening doors for provinces, who assume a pivotal part in answering environmental change and reducing public discharge levels through the organization of clean energy. Many draw in and cooperate with neighborhood utilities in energy arrangements, including utility-scale sustainable power projects, key administrative issues, framework modernization and capacity and energy confirmation techniques.

Further, the regulation incorporates a few estimates connected with medical care, including covering personal expenses of physician-endorsed drugs for Medicare recipients every year at $2,000,000.

The regulation was passed by the United States Senate on August 7 under the budget compromise process, which allows the Senate to avoid the delay and pass legislation with a simple majority vote if it meets a series of monetary requirements.The U.S. House is supposed to consider and pass the regulation on August 12.

The IRA has critical interests in energy and the environment. The regulation would:

Boost the venture tax break (ITC) and the creation tax reduction (PTC) for projects that start development before January 1, 2025. The PTC is a per kilowatt-hour (kWh) government tax reduction for sustainable power created by both private and public elements. The ITC provides an expense impetus for project proprietors or financial backers, which can incorporate regions, to create energy from sustainable sources. The IRA further permits state and neighborhood legislatures, among other qualified substances, to get immediate installments from the central government rather than the ITC or PTC.

(4) Extend the carbon capture and sequestration (45Q) tax credit to projects that begin construction before January 1, 2033.The regulation would likewise bring down the carbon catch edges expected to fit the bill for the credit.

Reduce the maximum value reduction of 45Q tax breaks when used in relation to burden-free bonds from 50% to 15%.This reduction could make the new carbon catch bonds laid out in the Bipartisan Infrastructure Law more alluring and attainable for provinces. The IRA further permits state and nearby legislatures to get immediate installments from the national government in lieu of the credit.

Establish a number of award programs at the Environmental Protection Agency (EPA) and other organizations to reduce discharges in a variety of areas.Regions would be straightforwardly qualified to apply for subsidies under a large number of these projects, including a $3 billion serious award program to decrease air pollution at ports and a $7 billion cutthroat award program to give monetary help to low-paying and burdened networks to convey or profit from zero-discharge innovations.

Lay out a $3 billion Neighborhood Access and Equity Grant program at the Federal Highway Administration (FHWA) to further develop walkability and security, relieve negative natural effects, and back-arrange and limit building exercises in hindered networks, including districts. Regions, which assume a huge part in making networks more secure and more walkable and open, would apply straightforwardly to the Department of Transportation for financing under the program.

Require the Department of Interior (DOI) to hold an inland oil and gas rent deal in something like 4 months of giving new coastal breeze and sun-powered privileges. It would likewise expect

DOI to hold a seaward oil and gas rent offer of no less than 60 million sections of land in the year preceding giving seaward wind leases. The provinces support expanded oil and gas production in a manner that boosts the subsidizing surges of the eminence income for the motivations behind preservation, diversion, reclamation, and security of essential public assets.

Give $5 billion in awards to help cooperative vegetation across the board, reforestation and perilous fill decrease tasks to work on the soundness of government and non-administrative forestlands. Provinces assume a functioning part in safeguarding the soundness of the backwoods through hearty vegetation executives.

Money and Tax Provisions

The IRA is projected to lessen shortfalls through the help of inflationary tensions. These counterbalances incorporate two significant expense arrangements:

Reinforcing the Internal Revenue Service's (IRS) charge requirement and consistence capacities by giving $80 billion to IRS citizen administrations, authorization endeavors, task backing, and business framework modernization.

A 15% elective least expense (AMT) for organizations with more than $1 billion in benefits.This arrangement would become compelling beginning in the 2023 fiscal year and includes an exception for organizations with confidential value.

However, unlike the Build Back Better Act, the IRA excludes relief from the $10,000 cap on state and local tax (SALT) derivation established in the 2017 Tax Cuts and Jobs Act.The House-passed bill would have raised the SALT cap to $80,000 and would have broadened the cap past its 2025 lapse date as a spending offset. NACo upholds the full deductibility of all state and neighborhood charges, especially the local charge, in the government charge code.

Wellbeing Provisions

The IRA incorporates a few arrangements connected with medical care that would influence districts, including:

It covers the personal expense of doctor-prescribed drugs for Medicare recipients every year at $2,000. We, as proprietors and administrators of the frameworks of care in our networks, support different techniques to aid cost control for physician-recommended drugs. Seniors and people with handicaps who can get physician endorsed drugs at a decreased rate under Medicare are bound to have better wellbeing results and are less inclined to be admitted into provincial wellbeing offices, for example, clinics and the trauma center.

It gives free antibodies to Medicare recipients which incorporate COVID-19 immunizations, shingles and other important immunizations. Districts, as key suppliers of nearby general wellbeing administrations and cutting-edge specialist co-ops for the medically helpless, continue to direct basic immunizations to occupants, regardless of their protection status.Government support for the expense of managing COVID-19 antibodies and other significant inoculations increases public insurance from irresistible sicknesses while diminishing the expense of uncompensated clinical consideration.

expands Affordable Care Act (ACA) premium appropriations to 2025, which help low-pay people with acquiring health care coverage on the ACA commercial center by covering how much a person pays for protection in view of their pay level. Significant for districts, these appropriations permit low-pay people to acquire reasonable health care coverage in light of their pay, decreasing the number of uninsured and medicinally impoverished people looking for care in provincial wellbeing offices. The sponsorships are set to lapse toward the end of 2022 and would be reached out for quite some time under this bill.

Prominently, not at all like the Build Back Better Act, the IRA does exclude the authorization of the Medicaid Reentry Act, which changes the Federal Medicaid Inmate Exclusion strategy (MIEP) by approving imprisoned people to get services covered by Medicaid 30 days before their release from prison or jail.

The impact of the expansion follows up on Americans.

Senate Majority Leader Chuck Schumer, D-N.Y., leaves a news meeting at the U.S. Legislative Hall on Friday, where he addressed journalists about the Inflation Reduction Act.

The huge environment, medical services, and assessment bill advancing to President Biden's work area is known as the Inflation Reduction Act. In any case, what difference does it make in slowing shopper costs, which are rising at the fastest rate in 40 years?

Following quite a while of discussions, a 730-page rendition of the bill passed the House on Friday, and President Biden said he intends to sign it into regulation one week from now.

Leftists passed a major environmental, welfare, and tax bill.This is what's in it.

Governmental view

The White House says the bundle will address expansion in two key ways: by bringing down energy and medical care costs for families and by assisting with cutting down the shortfall.

"Furthermore, that is the reason even Democrats and Republicans, previous Treasury secretaries, financial specialists in all cases have said that this bill will have a constructive outcome on expansion while additionally handling probably the greatest and well established issues confronting our nation, similar to professionally prescribed medications and like handling environmental change," said Brian Deese, overseer of the National Economic

Council, in a meeting this week with NPR's Morning Edition.

While specialists for the most part concur that the regulation will unassumingly assist with easing back the development of costs, it may not do as such in the ways you think, or as fast. Here are a few responses about how the regulation affects expansion.

Chapter 3; How might this bill cut down on expansion?

According to Shai Akabas, the Bipartisan Policy Center's director of financial strategy, the bill will make little progress toward restoring normalcy to the economy.

"It will generally work in the right direction and help the Federal Reserve, which has the critical obligation of snagging expansion," Akabas said.

ECONOMY

What's causing expansion?

As indicated by Akabas, there are three principal ways the bill targets rising costs. To begin with, it intends to reduce the government deficit, which is the contrast between how much the U.S. government spends and the amount it makes in assessments and income. Akabas said that at the point when there's less cash drifting in the economy, there will in general be less interest and lower cost climbs.

Since there are a few arrangements to energize spending in the bill, the net effect on expansion is muddled.

Second, it will advance the development of specific merchandise, mostly in sustainable power. He added that having a larger stockpile than requested could help to reduce certain costs in the long run.

Third, and all the more straightforwardly, one arrangement of the bill will assist in restricting the value development of specific doctor-prescribed drugs by permitting Medicare to arrange their expense with drug organizations. In any case, the absolute greatest drivers of expansion, including food and energy costs, are not quickly tended to.

So, when will it be?

The proposition won't assist in checking expansion emphatically or immediately, specialists say.

"It's not likely to significantly affect expansion in the next couple of months," Akabas said.

A few specialists, like Kent Smetters, staff head of the Penn Wharton Budget Model, don't anticipate a huge effect in the next couple of years.

"On one hand, it doesn't add to expansion, which was the past worry that individuals had about passing regulations like this at the present time," Smetters said. However, at a similar token, it doesn't exactly detract from the ascent in costs.

The objective Congressional Budget Office, which scored the bill, likewise resolved that the bill will have an "insignificant impact" on expansion this year and next.

In the event that the effect on expansion is restricted, what else does it do?

The bundle includes $369 billion for new spending to decrease ozone-depleting substance discharges, put resources into clean energy innovations and broaden appropriations for the Affordable Care Act.

The bill likewise plans to get more than $300 billion in new income, Democrats say, by forcing a 15% minimum duty on partnerships making more than $1 billion and through another excise charge on corporate stock buybacks.

"The method for contemplating this isn't about expansion by any stretch of the imagination, however about the tradeoffs between aiding individuals who need more assistance, particularly in medical services and lessening carbon, versus the likely effect on future speculation," Smetters said.

What are a few changes I'll find sooner rather than later?

While specialists don't see a fast track to expansion through this bill, there are a scope of measures to assist with significant expenses. For example,

Expansion and environmental change are handled in a new Senate bargain that Biden calls "notable."

Legislative perspective.

Expansion and environmental change are handled in a new Senate bargain that Biden calls "notable."

The bill offers various tax reductions for individuals switching to cleaner energy sources, including electric vehicles and housetop sunlight-powered chargers. Those motivators will produce results in 2023, and as per Democrats, will mean a 40% cut in nursery discharges from 2005 levels before the decade's over.

The Internal Revenue Service will get a lift in financing, especially to further develop its client support and expense implementation. Akabas said that speculation could assist with easing a portion of the difficulties with long reaction times or getting charge discounts handled. It may also expand the number of charges that are currently owed but are ignored.

A large number of Americans will keep on profiting from endowments that assist with rising medical coverage charges that were initially scheduled to lapse one year from now.

The bill will set a $2,000 yearly limit for personal physician-recommended drugs for individuals protected by Medicare, which will be generally significant for senior residents with diseases like malignant growth and multiple sclerosis. Yet, that arrangement will not emerge until 2025.

"Costs are high presently, but we're discussing costs that have been putting trouble on family spending plans for a really long time," said Rakeen Mabud, the central financial specialist of the Groundwork Collaborative, an ever-evolving financial aspects think tank.

"We've been battling with soaring medical care costs for quite a while, and this bill is a significant step in the right direction."

Am I going to see an expansion in my duties?

It's improbable that a larger percentage of families will see an immediate effect on their charges, said Akabas, who centers around government spending plan strategy.

All things being equal, the duty increments will, to a great extent, fall on partnerships. That being said, a few workers might feel that taxation rate in a roundabout way.

Akabas made sense of it by assuming an organization was less productive and less ready to burn through cash on work and less willing to pay higher wages. "At that point, that will be felt by people all throughout the economy," Akabas made sense of it.

Chye-Ching Huang, the leader overseer of the Tax Law Center at New York University, doesn't anticipate a huge effect on compensation. Huang said that since the tax reduction in 2017, financial specialists didn't see a significant distinction in compensation.

She said. "Switching a portion of that for the exceptionally biggest companies can be anticipated to have a comparably small or intangible impact."

The Senate-passed Inflation Reduction Act (IRA), a replacement to the House-passed Build Back Better Act of late 2021, has been promoted by President

Biden to, among other things, assist with lessening the nation's devastating expansion. Utilizing the Tax Foundation's General Equilibrium Model, we gauge that the Inflation Reduction Act would decrease long-term monetary results by around 0.2 percent and dispose of around 29,000 full-time identical positions in the United States. It would likewise diminish normal after-charge salaries for citizens across each pay quintile for a really long time.

By diminishing long-run financial development, this bill may really demolish expansion by obliging the useful limit of the economy.

Our examination contains evaluations of the monetary, financial, and distributional effects of the Inflation Reduction Act as determined in the bill text that was changed and passed in the Senate on August 7.

Utilizing the General Equilibrium Model, we gauge that the duty arrangements, IRS implementation, and medication valuation arrangements in the bill would increase government income by about $676 billion over the spending plan window, prior to representing $352 billion in extended tax reductions for people and organizations, bringing about a net income increment of about $324 billion from 2022 to 2031.

Barring the expected income from expanded charge consistence and the medication estimating arrangements, the bill would lose about $84 billion in income over the financial plan window.

On the duty arrangements influencing you.

Purchase to have experiences from our trusted experts delivered directly to your inbox.

Section 4 : Economical Impacts of the Expansion on the Tax Foundation General Equilibrium Model, August 2022.

The Senate-passed Inflation Reduction Act (IRA), a replacement to the House-passed Build Back Better Act of late 2021, has been promoted by President Biden to, among other things, assist with decreasing the nation's devastating expansion. Utilizing the Tax Foundation's General Equilibrium Model, we gauge that the Inflation Reduction Act would diminish long-term financial results by around 0.2 percent and kill around 29,000 full-time comparable positions in the United States. It would likewise reduce normal after-charge livelihoods for citizens across each pay quintile over an extended period of time.

By diminishing long-run monetary development, this bill may really demolish expansion by obliging the useful limit of the economy.

Our examination contains appraisals of the monetary, financial, and distributional effects of the Inflation Reduction Act as determined in the bill text that was corrected and passed in the Senate on August 7.

Utilizing the General Equilibrium Model, we gauge that the duty arrangements, IRS implementation, and medication valuation arrangements in the bill would increase government income by about $676 billion over the spending plan window, prior to representing $352 billion in extended tax reductions for people and organizations, bringing about a net income increment of about $324 billion from 2022 to 2031.

Barring the expected income from expanded charge consistence and the medication valuing arrangements, the bill would lose about $84 billion in income over the financial plan window.

extends the extended health care coverage Premium Tax Credits given in the American Rescue Plan Act (ARPA), including permitting higher-pay families to fit the bill for the credits and helping the sponsorship for lower-pay families, through the end of 2025.

Chapter 4; Effects on Corporate and international taxes

forces a 15% reduction in corporate book pay for enterprises with benefits exceeding $1 billion, effective for charge years beginning after December 31, 2022.

makes a 1% extract charge on the value of stock repurchased during the available year, minus new stock issuances, effective for repurchases after December 31, 2022.Rejected from the assessment are stocks added to retirement records, benefits, and worker stock possession plans (ESOPs).

changes, expands, and makes an assortment of tax breaks for environmentally friendly power, energy, and different endeavors essentially through 2031 or 2033.

raises the Superfund charge on raw petroleum and imported petrol to 16.4 pennies per barrel (listed to expansion) and increments different expenses and charges on the non-renewable energy source area.

It also expands the exploration and advancement tax break sum that can be asserted against finance charges for independent ventures by $250,000.

Financial Effects

While the most recent proposition avoids a portion of the significant duty rate increments contained in the House-passed Build Back Better Act, this proposition would increase government rates on work and speculation, disincentivizing useful movement. We estimate that the Inflation Reduction Act will reduce long-term GDP by about 0.2 percent.

The bill would reduce long-run American livelihoods (as measured by gross national product, or GNP) by less than 0.05 percent.The bill's decrease in the spending plan shortage over an extended time period shows GNP at around 0.1 percent, but this is balanced by a somewhat more noteworthy than 0.1 percent decline in GNP from the duty increments. The bill would decrease the capital stock by around 0.3 percent and wages by around 0.1 percent, while killing around 29,000 full-time comparable positions.

The proposed 15% tax on corporate book pay is the most financially damaging provision in the bill, reducing GDP by 0.1 percent and costing approximately 20,000 jobs.While it now excludes accelerated deterioration, tax breaks, and various other things, the book charge remains a significant duty increment on corporate pay as it hits a few other book-charge contrasts and limits the capacity to convey forward losses.The excise charge on stock buybacks likewise wipes out around 7,000 positions.

For reasons for assessing the bill's effect on government financial plan deficiencies, interest installments, and coming changes in GNP, we utilized gauges from the Congressional Budget Office (CBO) demonstrating about $150 billion in extra spending over the spending plan window

(2022 to 2031), notwithstanding scored charge arrangements.

We estimate that the bill would result in a $224 billion decrease in the deficit (including revenue installments) in the first decade and continue to decrease shortfalls after that, resulting in a decrease in payments to unfamiliar owners of the public obligation and a 0.1 percent expansion in long run GNP.We treat the nontax expenses as moving installments with no related effect on the economy over the long haul.

Gross income is decreased by about $352 billion in tax reductions, which comes to about $324 billion in expanded income net of tax breaks.

We depended on gauges given by the JCT and the CBO for arrangements we didn't demonstrate. The bill remembers about $150 billion for extra spending, and when joined with the $352 billion in tax breaks, the bill increases spending by about $502 billion over 10 years.

The biggest duty arrangement is the 15% minimum assessment on corporate book pay for organizations with normal yearly changed budget summary pay that surpasses $1 billion for any three successive earlier fiscal years, with a viable start in 2023. While we gauge that the arrangement raises $153 billion over the spending plan window, this might be an upper bound, as it represents no social reactions — that is, aversion — since the design of the expense is exceptional. Genuine income could be less if, for example, organizations answer by diminishing revealed monetary pay.

A 1% excise tax on stock repurchases made by domestic public companies is a second source of revenue.We gauge that this arrangement would raise $48 billion over the course of the next 10 years.

On a unique premise—that is, representing the diminished size of the economy coming about because of the expense increments—we gauge the bill would bring in a total of about $308 billion in income net of tax breaks over the course of the next ten year.

The Senate-passed Inflation Reduction Act (IRA), a replacement to the House-passed Build Back Better Act of late 2021, has been promoted by President Biden to, among other things, assist with lessening the nation's devastating expansion. Utilizing the Tax Foundation's General Equilibrium Model, we gauge that the Inflation Reduction Act would diminish long-term financial results by around 0.2 percent and dispense with around 29,000 full-time identical positions in the United States. It would likewise decrease normal after-charge wages for citizens across each pay quintile for a really long time.

This bill may really deteriorate long-run monetary development by obliging the useful limit of the economy.

Our examination contains evaluations of the monetary, financial, and distributional effects of the Inflation Reduction Act as determined in the bill text that was revised and passed in the Senate on August 7.

Utilizing the General Equilibrium Model, we gauge that the expense arrangements, IRS requirements, and medication valuation arrangements in the bill would increase government income by about $676 billion over the spending plan window, prior to representing $352 billion in extended tax reductions for people and organizations, bringing about a net income increment of about $324 billion from 2022 to 2031.

Barring the expected income from expanded charge consistence and the medication valuation arrangements, the bill would lose about $84 billion in income over the spending plan window.

extends the extended health care coverage Premium Tax Credits given in the American Rescue Plan Act (ARPA), including permitting higher-pay families to fit the bill for the credits and helping the sponsorship for lower-pay families, through the end of 2025.

Corporate and international taxes

imposes a 15% duty on corporate book pay for companies with benefits exceeding $1 billion, effective for charge years beginning after December 31, 2022.

For repurchases after December 31, 2022, a 1% extraction charge is applied to the value of stock repurchased during the available year, net of new stock issuances.Stocks added to retirement accounts, annuities, and worker stock ownership plans (ESOPs) are excluded from the expense.

It imposes a 95 percent excise tax on drug manufacturers in order to reduce drug costs.

It also expands the examination and improvement tax reduction sum that can be asserted against finance charges for independent ventures by $250,000.

The bill would reduce long-run American earnings (as measured by gross national product, or GNP) by less than 0.05 percent.The bill's decrease in the spending plan deficiency over an extended time period shows GNP to be down by around 0.1 percent, but this is counterbalanced by a marginally more prominent than 0.1 percent decline in GNP from the duty increments. The bill would reduce the capital stock by approximately 0.3 percent and wages by approximately 0.1 percent, while eliminating approximately 29,000 full-time equivalent positions.

The proposed 15% minimum assessment on corporate book pay is the most economically damaging provision in the bill, reducing GDP by 0.1 percent and costing approximately 20,000 jobs.While it now excludes accelerated deterioration, tax cuts, and various other things, the book charge remains a significant expense increment on corporate pay as it hits a few other book-charge contrasts and limits the capacity to convey forward misfortunes.The excise charge on stock buybacks additionally takes out around 7,000 positions.

For reasons of assessing the bill's effect on government financial plan shortfalls, interest installments, and coming changes in GNP, we utilized gauges from the Congressional Budget Office (CBO) showing about $150 billion in extra spending over the financial plan window (2022 to 2031), notwithstanding scored charge arrangements.

We estimate that the bill would result in a $224 billion decrease in the deficit (including revenue installments) in the first decade and continue to decrease shortfalls after that, resulting in a decrease in payments to unfamiliar owners of the public obligation and a 0.1 percent expansion in long run GNP.We treat the nontax expenses as moving installments with no related effect on the economy over the long haul.

The effects on income

On a traditional premise, the House bill would bring about $324 billion in government income from 2022 to 2031. The bill contains about $676 billion in gross income raisers and contains about

$213 billion in corporate duty increments, $54 billion in individual expense increments, $130 billion net from extra IRS charge authorization, $278 billion from the medication estimating arrangements, and about $1.1 billion in net income from things scored by the Joint Committee on Taxation (JCT).

Gross income is diminished by about $352 billion in tax reductions, coming to about $324 billion in expanded income net of tax breaks.

We depended on gauges given by the JCT and the CBO for arrangements we didn't make. The bill appropriates about $150 billion for extra spending, and when joined with the $352 billion in tax reductions, the bill increments spending by about $502 billion over the next 10 years.

The biggest expense arrangement is the 15% minimum assessment on corporate book pay for companies with normal yearly changed fiscal summary pay that surpasses $1 billion for any three sequential earlier fiscal years, with a compelling start in 2023. While we gauge that the arrangement raises $153 billion over the financial plan window, this might be an upper bound, as it represents no social reactions—that is, evasion—since the design of the expense is special. Genuine income could be less if, for example, organizations answer by diminishing revealed monetary pay.

A 1% excise tax on stock repurchases made by domestic public companies is a second source of revenue.We gauge that this arrangement would raise $48 billion over the course of the next ten years.

On a unique premise—that is, representing the decreased size of the economy coming about because of the expense increments—we gauge the bill would bring in all of about $308 billion in income net of tax reductions over the course of the next ten years.

assessed burning through for effort and wellbeing arrangements scored by the Congressional Budget Office and adapted to $5 billion in dry spell flexibility financing added by the Senate. Negative shortfall figures show an expansion in the spending plan shortage.

The income table likewise presents the income influence from 2023 to 2032. Over the course of the next 10 years, we gauge that the Inflation Reduction Act will bring about $385 billion in customary income and about $361 billion progressively subsequent to that, representing monetary effects.

The effect of distributional

Over an extended period, the Inflation Reduction Act would raise negligible personal expense rates paid by higher workers and companies. The distributional outcomes that follow do exclude the effect of medication estimating arrangements or IRS requirements on after-charge earnings.

The recommendations would increase the after-charge pay of the base quintile by around 2.1 percent in 2023 on a customary premise, to a great extent because of extended medical care endowments. The top 1% of workers would see a 0.1 percent increase in after-tax pay in 2023, thanks to extended energy tax breaks that offset decreased earnings from corporate bookkeeping duty and share repurchases.